T0385476

• *Affirmations for Turbulent Times* •

AFFIRMATIONS FOR

Resonant Words to Soothe Body and Mind

TURBULENT TIMES

SARAH PEYTON

A Norton Professional Book
New York • *London*

This volume is intended as a general information resource, not as a substitute for medical advice; no remedy, strategy, or suggestion described in these pages should be used in lieu of individualized attention from a qualified professional. As of press time, the URLs displayed in this book link or refer to existing websites. The publisher is not responsible for, and should not be deemed to endorse or recommend, any website other than its own or any content available on the Internet (including, without limitation, any website, blog page, or information page) that is not created by W.W. Norton. The author, similarly, is not responsible for third-party material.

Copyright © 2022 by Sarah Peyton

All rights reserved
Printed in the United States of America
First Edition

For information about permission to reproduce selections from this book, write to Permissions, W. W. Norton & Company, Inc., 500 Fifth Avenue, New York, NY 10110

For information about special discounts for bulk purchases, please contact W. W. Norton Special Sales at specialsales@wwnorton.com or 800-233-4830

Manufacturing by Versa Press
Book design by Judith Stagnitto Abbate / Abbate Design
Production manager: Katelyn MacKenzie

Library of Congress Cataloging-in-Publication Data

Names: Peyton, Sarah, 1962- author.
Title: Affirmations for turbulent times : resonant words to soothe body and mind / Sarah Peyton.
Description: First edition. | New York : W.W. Norton & Company, [2022] | Includes bibliographical references and index.
Identifiers: LCCN 2021008989 | ISBN 9781324019619 (hardcover) | ISBN 9781324019626 (epub)
Subjects: LCSH: Affirmations. | Peace of mind.
Classification: LCC BF697.5.S47 P49 2022 | DDC 158.1--dc23
LC record available at https://lccn.loc.gov/2021008989

W. W. Norton & Company, Inc., 500 Fifth Avenue, New York, N.Y. 10110
www.wwnorton.com

W. W. Norton & Company Ltd., 15 Carlisle Street, London W1D 3BS

2 3 4 5 6 7 8 9 0

CONTENTS

Welcome and Introduction to the Affirmations   ix

THEME 1 ✧ Living with Chaos and Uncertainty

- Nostalgia   2
- Unpredictability   4
- Irritability   6
- Fears and impacts   8
- Fear of the "new normal"   10
- Helplessness and panic   12

THEME 2 ✧ Health and Well-Being

- Health and sickness   16
- Needing comfort when you are sick   18
- Aging   20
- Eating worries   22
- Always being tired or fatigued   24
- Drinking to manage turbulent times   26
- Not being able to be physically active   28
- Living with long-term illness   30

THEME 3 ◈ Loneliness and Community

- Isolation and loneliness   34
- Too many people in too little space   36
- Nostalgia for a stopped world   38
- Guilt about loving solitude   40
- Waiting for someone who doesn't come   42
- Leftovers from the pandemic   44

THEME 4 ◈ Work and Contribution

- Work and money   48
- Too much work   50
- Making mistakes   52
- When people aren't contributing   54
- When people are always working   56
- Burnout   58

THEME 5 ◈ Family and Home

- Responsibility   62
- Good parenting   64
- Domestic conflict   66
- Care for aging parents   68
- Family disagreements   70
- Sickness and death   72

THEME 6 ◈ Mourning Our Losses

- Missing the people without names   76
- Friends   78

- Adventure and travel   80
- Intimacy   82
- Opportunities for growth   84
- Those who have died   86

THEME 7 ◇ Loving the Planet

- The climate crisis   90
- Losing our planetary home   92
- The ecosystems   94
- The bumblebees   96
- Indestructible nature   98
- World peace   100

THEME 8 ◇ Emotions and Longings

- Fear   104
- Anger   106
- Grief   108
- Disgust and contempt   110
- Desires and longings   112
- Perfectionism and shame   114

THEME 9 ◇ Living the Creative Life

- Writer's or creative block   118
- Deadlines   120
- Missing collaboration   122
- Creation shame   124
- Social media distraction   126
- Creating something you love   128

THEME 10 ◆ Caring for Our Energy

- Boredom and meaning   132
- Deep fatigue   134
- The cost of addiction   136
- Being unable to sleep   138
- Worrying and energy   140
- Social media's effects   142

THEME 11 ◆ Helplessness and Choice

- Wanting choice   146
- Public policies   148
- Envy of others   150
- Technology   152
- Everything feeling out of control   154
- Financial dependence   156

THEME 12 ◆ Stepping into Celebration

- Celebrating when times are so turbulent   160
- Accomplishment   162
- A good day   164
- Being loved   166
- Brain change   168
- Affirmations   170

Twelve Final Invitations   172
Author's Closing: What Next?   175
Notes   178

Welcome and Introduction to the Affirmations

UMAN BRAINS can be a little difficult to make peace with. Depending on how much aloneness and emotional trauma we have lived through, our brains may have picked up the habits of relentless self-criticism and self-blame. Unfortunately, although these habits are well intended and are meant to improve us and make us safe, they don't actually contribute to our long-term well-being. Instead, these thought patterns increase our anxiety and stress levels, depress our immune systems, and keep us from fully engaging in the world.

The good news is that with resonance—the powerful combination of understanding and warmth—brains change. With resonance, our brains become good and welcoming places for us to live. Supportive neurotransmitters start to flow, improving mood, energy, and relationships. Relentless self-criticism and self-blame fall away, replaced by effectiveness, new capacity to focus, and new abilities to dream and to rest. This change happens thought by thought, and neural connection by neural connection.

This means that the thoughts we have about ourselves, our lives, and our futures matter. The words we use with ourselves make a difference. "Oh, so simple!" we might think. "All I have to do is change the words I use with myself." That is partly true, but if we use words that are entirely contradictory to our feelings, it is stressful for us. So there is a negotiation between acknowledging what we truly feel, which might include grief, anger, shame, or fear, and the kinds of words that nourish the growth of neurons— the ones that make our brains good places to live and that support our resiliency.

One way to use words that nourish the growth of support-ive neurons is to create affirmations—positive expressions that encourage deep self-acceptance, self-warmth, calm ground-edness, and hope. This book offers you a series of affirmations which you can use as starting points for the creation of powerful acknowledgments and statements to change your brain.

Research shows us that we find affirmations pleasurable and that they light up the brain's reward system. Of course, we do actually have to enjoy them for this to happen. An important ele-ment of finding satisfaction in affirmations is to make sure that we have our own consent to work with them. Take a moment right now to ask yourself: Is it okay for me to invite a positive point of view of myself and the world? Am I willing to acknowledge the ways in which things have been difficult? Am I also willing to take responsibility for the ways in which my brain's inner voice has been negative, and reach for something a little more hopeful and supportive? Am I willing to let words help to restore my sense of self-competence and connect me to my deepest values? If possible, explicitly give yourself permission to try this approach to self-support and see how it works for you.

Once you receive your own consent to move forward, the activation of the brain's reward center can decrease pain and allow different thoughts about the future. Affirmations can also change the way the brain thinks about itself. They have been shown to help people move out of immobilization into action, decrease stress, increase well-being, and improve academic performance.

The book is divided into 12 themes related to the turbulent times in which we are living. Each of these themes has 6 or so different subjects that address different aspects of the themes. You will see questions on the left-hand page and traditional affirmations on the right-hand page. The questions, or wonderings, support the exploration of each theme. You will answer yes to some of the questions and no to others. Researchers have found that asking yourself questions, even using your own first name when you do it, helps your brain to orient toward the self in ways that calm you. If the questions don't feel right, make sure to ask other questions that do feel right, to help you relax and receive the affirmations even more fully. People find different ways of using the affirmations. I recommend that you experiment to find out when and how often the affirmations are most helpful to you. The times when we are most vulnerable to the automatic voice of the brain are the times that I most enjoy using affirmations: in the morning when waking; during morning and evening self-care rituals; when driving or washing dishes; when standing in line. You can experiment with post-it notes on mirrors, with taking phone photos of your favorite affirmations so that you can review them when you are out running errands, or with keeping the book by your bedside. If there is one sentence that is most powerful to you, use that sentence. If the whole page relaxes your body the most, use the whole page. You may find that you work on one theme over time, or that you open the book randomly in the morning to support your day. You won't be able to tell what most supports you until you experiment and find out.

As you move into the book, you may find that you aren't even sure it's okay to feel the feelings that are named. Everyone has emotions that seem too big for them, or times when it seems like too many emotions are happening at once. These limits come from the worlds we live in, and they make sense. Humans need to have belonging in each of their worlds, and part of the way we belong is to feel the same way, and in the same amounts, as others in our groups. This book offers you your own community of feeling, a safe space to notice and name your own real experience of these turbulent times. If possible, give yourself permission to name what is true for you as you read, and to feel what you really feel. This will support you in getting more out of the book.

Theme 1

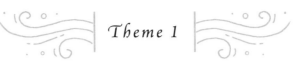

LIVING WITH CHAOS AND UNCERTAINTY

NOSTALGIA

Wonderings

ARE YOU MISSING your relatively peaceful life before the present tumultuous times? Do you miss only having to worry about things that were personal, instead of having to worry for the whole world? Do you ache for the old, thoughtless movement through your days, without having to carefully assess every action for danger to self and loved ones, or harm to the ecosystems of the world? Are there moments when you would love nothing more than a return to innocence, even if your innocence was actually ignorance? And at the same time, do you really want the world to be better, rather than only pretending that it is better? Do you support changes that would reduce systemic injustice and make sure that every voice mattered?

Affirmations

GIVE MYSELF REST, and let myself fully rest, in the world as it is. I embrace the present moment for the truth of its tumult and still find rejuvenation in my breath. I claim my life during these tumultuous times as my own regular life, and I support myself in having times when I only worry about my personal experience. I also give myself moments to worry about the world and everyone in it, and moments when I do not worry at all. I acknowledge that my personal life is bound up in the life of the world, and I affirm that my worry stems from love of life. I tune in to what matters and allow myself to work for change, and to be nourished by life itself, by love itself.

UNPREDICTABILITY

Wonderings

IS UNPREDICTABILITY HARD on you? Do you need to know what's happening so that you can imagine yourself into the future? If you long for predictability, do you need to remember the predictability of your own beating heart? Do you have a need to be able to use the present moment as certainty enough to help you move forward? When you realize that one minute from now you may still be sitting here reading, or that you can at least predict that much of the future, does your body relax, knowing that you can know the next minute? And as you feel into the next hour, can you see a bit of what will happen, and does your body relax with a tiny bit of predictability? You may have some sense that you can see into tomorrow, too, and with that, is there a kind of relaxation, a reassurance?

MAY NOT be able to know what the future will bring, but I consent to my resonating self being there waiting for me. I will meet the future and myself there, whatever happens, with my own compassion, understanding, and warmth. I send myself into the future to meet me at the edge of my not knowing. I hold my own hand as we step into the not knowing, and I have faith in my own capacity to bring my strengths and gifts to meet it all, whatever comes.

IRRITABILITY

Wonderings

ARE YOU CONTINUALLY FRUSTRATED with what's happening around you? Do you wish the world flowed smoothly? But is flow so unlikely that naming it is like naming an impossible dream? Do the interruptions and setbacks and failures of this life make you feel like you are going crazy? Are you exhausted by your own relentless dissatisfaction? Do you worry that all these frustrations are happening because you aren't enough, and that if only you were a different person, everything would go smoothly? Do you wish you had a stage manager behind the scenes of your life who could keep track of the props and iron out the kinks in the movement of things? Do you wish that you didn't even notice the blocks to your flow? If not noticing blocks and simply moving through them is too impossible, do you instead wish for an infinite supply of patience?

Affirmations

HAVE AFFECTION and warmth for myself, even when I am irritated with the blocks and obstructions in my life. I appreciate my own love of flow and my desire for everything to run smoothly. I breathe into my irritation, feeling the crackle of subterranean rage, and I let it point me toward what I love. I acknowledge my exhaustion, and I invite myself to move as slowly as I need to move, and to breathe as deeply as I need to breathe, remembering that roadblocks are just obstructions rather than symbols of life threat.

FEARS AND IMPACTS

Wonderings

DO SOME of the things other people do, and the decisions they make, sometimes frighten you? Are you scared by people's thoughtlessness? Would you love to live in a world where everyone thought about the impact they had on others? Where there was mutual consideration? A world where people even noticed that their fears impact others? Sometimes does that seem so impossible that you would even like to live in a world that didn't have other people in it? Would you love, just for one day, to experience a world filled with kindness, conscious awareness, imagination, and generosity?

Affirmations

 **AM CENTERED AND GROUNDED,** even when others are not. I come from a calm place in the middle of my being where I can be aware without having to be hypervigilant. I am willing to be loved by humans in all their irritating desire to have others do what they want, and I am willing to love them in return. When people are taking actions that I consider dangerous or controlling, I remove myself whenever that is possible. I have choices about how quickly I move and about whether I stop and wait for other people or dangerous circumstances to pass. I make myself and my safety important to me, and I move with patience, lightness, fluidity, and a sense of humor.

FEAR OF THE "NEW NORMAL"

Wonderings

WHEN THE WORLD is turned upside down with stress and trauma and then settles into a "new normal," do you wish for the new to be better than the old? Do you worry about the way things are settling? Are there worries about losses—of liberty, choice, thoughtfulness, and flexibility? Do you wish for a return of trust? Just for a moment, would you like to be able to believe the old narrative that all changes are for the better? And when you see losses that leave us in worse shape, do the cells of your body protest the changes? Do you long to see human creativity and generosity actually show up and shape our future?

Affirmations

SEE THE PRESENT TIME with clear eyes and calm thoughts, understanding what is happening, even when I don't like it. I am a part of this world, no matter how things unfold, and my voice matters. I speak about what is important to me with love, power, and gentleness. In the places where I make decisions, I use my decisions to create a world that has the values that are important to me. Every moment is an opportunity to create my world.

HELPLESSNESS AND PANIC

Wonderings

ARE YOU SOMETIMES flooded with the stress that comes from helplessness, as you realize that one of the only things you can do is nothing? Are you trying to take action when there is no action to be taken? Do your arms want to be able to move, contribute, take care of things, and yet there's nothing to do? When a lot of people's lives are at stake, do you become more and more worried, more concerned, more anxious, more tender? Is the scale of things going wrong inconceivably huge and impossible to digest? Do you need a sense of being able to step out of time, to be able to leave it entirely?

Affirmations

OR THIS MOMENT, I deliberately step out of the stress and take a deep breath that moves out into my arms and legs, and reassures my body. I remember that the actions of being here, taking care of the people I love, taking action where possible, tending to people who need support, and caring for myself all bring me agency and meaning. Even when there is helplessness, the action of accompaniment of self or other is a real contribution. Just for this moment, I breathe in freedom and choice, and I let myself take an action to protect or nourish myself or another.

Living with Chaos and Uncertainty

Theme 2

HEALTH AND

WELL-BEING

HEALTH AND SICKNESS

Wonderings

WHEN YOU ARE WORRIED about your health, does everything seem like sickness? Do you worry that headaches and skin rashes are cancer? Are you on high alert for any signs that you might be ill? Do you love your lungs and your heart and your brain and your immune system—and do you want to keep them safe? Do you feel helpless and do you want to have complete control over your environment? When you are worried, do you take your temperature every hour? Do you find yourself washing your hands more than you need to? Sometimes, do you have trouble thinking any other thoughts besides ruminations on the dread of getting sick? Would it be sweet to be able to rest from your own worries? Do you wish for some kind of super immunity that would give you confidence and certainty and invulnerability to the ills of this world?

Affirmations

FOR THIS MOMENT, I know my own essential wellness. I feel grateful to my immune system for its attention and care about invaders, and I embrace the knowledge that my own relaxation supports my immune system even more than my hypervigilance does. I have patience and care for my fears, and I stay with myself, even when I am scared of getting sick. I stand beside myself and hold my own hand in support through this difficult time. I allow myself to feel into the depths below my fears and find my grief at the state of the world and at my own vulnerability. I release the pressure that is fueling the fear and I let a deep acceptance of "what is" coexist with a conscientious and practical self-care.

NEEDING COMFORT WHEN YOU ARE SICK

Wonderings

WHEN YOU ARE SICK are you uncomfortable? Is being sick a little like having sand in your nervous system? Are you in pain? Does your skin hurt? Do your joints and your eyes ache? Is it hard to have any sense of being rejuvenated from rest when there is no comfort in rest? Do you need to be soothed? And sometimes does it seem like soothing isn't even possible? Does being sick come with the fear of not getting better, or of dying, especially in these times? Does it seem like every minute of being sick lasts forever, and is it hard to remember that people mostly get better from being sick? Would it be lovely to have an iron-clad guarantee that you will get better, and that this period of ill-health won't last long? And do you need patient and warm accompaniment as you travel through this illness?

I AM IN A WARM and mutually supportive relationship with my own immune system. Nothing is more helpful for immune systems than affection and interest and care, and I turn toward myself with the intention of having good feelings for myself. I ground myself in the knowledge that this moment is just one of many in my life, and that my life is much more than being sick. I anticipate a future where I feel better, and I call on hope to nourish me. If I have support from others, I am grateful for their presence, rather than irritated with their micro-failures. And when I am irritated, I have warmth and affection for my irritated self. Even in moments when I am sick, I am willing to remember that I have recovered from illness many times, and that this time, too, my system is healing, and that I am whole.

Health and Well-Being

AGING

Wonderings

ARE YOU DISTRACTED and discomforted and worried and mourning the losses that come with aging? Is it uncomfortable to notice the wobbly flesh, the graying and thinning hair, the poor sleep, the swollen ankles, the drying skin, the weariness, the stiffness, the aching joints, the increased vulnerability to infection, the loss of sharp eyesight, and the stooping posture? When you are suddenly reminded of these things, whether because of physical discomfort or from catching your reflection in a mirror or window, does the sense of loss and bewilderment ambush you? Are you confused about whether you are yourself for a moment? Do you wonder where you have disappeared to, and who is here now looking back at you?

RECOGNIZE MYSELF, no matter how much the way I look changes. I meet the losses that come with aging with warmth and humor. I remind myself of the beauty and richness that human brains gain with age, and of the softening of the attitude toward self. I remember that the process of aging is shared with all humans throughout time. My wisdom comes from relationship, love, and as much self-warmth as I can bring myself. My wisdom, my humor, and my love are my true rewards for living many years on this planet.

EATING WORRIES

Wonderings

ARE YOU ALWAYS HUNGRY, even though you don't know what you are hungry for? Whatever is wrong, will food be a remedy? Are you desperate for relief? Will food distract you from the world, even just for the instant that it is in your mouth? Will the crunch, the salt, the sweetness, and the fat take care of you, no matter what the people in your world are doing? Will it love you? Is it entirely dependable and available? Do you eat to push away the anxiety and the worry of not being able to do anything? Do you sometimes feel shame about your body, and is the shame so painful that you eat to lessen it, creating a terrible downward spiral? Is it impossible to make healthy choices, either because of the cravings or because of the disinterest? Do you ache for freedom and to always have choice?

NOTICE EACH WAY that food takes care of me. I release any agreements food has with me, or that I have with food, instead allowing myself to move, step by step, into freedom. Even when I don't have much interest in food, I'm willing to eat and to take into account what will nourish me. I lean into the echoes of unbearable emotions and loneliness from childhood, trusting my own adult heart to be big enough to hold me now. My hunger is for connection and for resonance, for emotional stability and support. Instead of eating for comfort, just for this moment, I hold myself snugly and warmly in my emotions, and I will allow all my emotions to make sense to me.

ALWAYS BEING TIRED
OR FATIGUED

Wonderings

ARE YOU WEARY? Do you feel bewildered about where to find the energy to support yourself? Is there so little to call upon, just what comes from not-very-restful sleep? Is it hard to decide what to use your little bit of energy for? Would you love to have some sense that you could count on building your strength bit by bit, and that it wouldn't all suddenly be gone? Is there a helplessness that needs to be named? Do you long to have access to stable, readily available strength and resilience? Each time you do have access to this energy, do you have to use much of it to mourn the life that you haven't been able to live and to see the impacts of long-term fatigue? And when you don't have those resources, might it be supportive to be able to tap into immense patience and gentleness for yourself?

ACKNOWLEDGE the enormous effort that I am exerting to keep myself going through this difficult time. I appreciate my rhythms—my breath, my heartbeat—and I feel the life energy in me, even when it is in low gear. I know myself as a living being, powered by life. I have affection for my own exhaustion, impatience, and irritation. I am my own ally and I am on my own side, even when I am not able to live the way I want to. I am gentle with myself and others as I find my way.

DRINKING TO MANAGE TURBULENT TIMES

Wonderings

ARE YOU LONGING for a different, more fun version of you? Are you wanting to drink alcohol, knowing that it will give you that first kick of goofy, warm euphoria that allows you to be you, but not you? Do you love the variety of the drinks and the fun that comes with the mixing? Do you count on the beer, the wine, the whisky, the vodka, to take away some of reality and offer you an easier version of life? And do you count on drinks to transform shame into ease? Is alcohol something you can have in the morning, at midday, in the evening, and at night so that you can check out, enjoy life, and feel a little pleasant dizziness?

FEEL GREAT WARMTH for my brain as it truly is, in the ways that it has been changed by the substances and behaviors that have had the promise of making me feel better. I love my brain even when it thinks it can solve my problems by drinking. I acknowledge the gravitational pull of this kind of problem solving, and I hold myself with care as I negotiate living in a new way. I have new options. I use resonance to respond to myself. I resource myself with sources greater than myself—nature, ancestors, or a sense of the divine—instead of thinking I have to handle everything on my own.

NOT BEING ABLE TO BE PHYSICALLY ACTIVE

Wonderings

ARE YOU FRUSTRATED and restless and tired, all at once? Are there changes in health, energy, geographic location, available time, or the movements of friends that have made you unable to move the way you are used to moving? Are you currently unable to find a way to run, walk, dance, swim, bicycle, play sports, or do exercise class? Are you simultaneously itchy for activity and exhausted from stress? If people have moved away or their circumstances have changed, do you miss the folks you used to work out with? Do you most like it when you can do the activities that suit your body, at the time that suits you, in company that you enjoy? Do you long to claim your own right to activity and self-care, no matter what the external circumstances are?

ACKNOWLEDGE THE CHANGES that the progression of my life brings, and the moves and losses that take me away from my health routines. I breathe deeply, in appreciation of my body and its resilience even during the times I can't take the care of it that I would like. I'm grateful to my body for sleeping, being awake, being hungry, eating, and for periods of rest. Even when my body doesn't want to move, I do not give up. Each day, I take some time to see if my body is willing to try new ways, new times, new company, or the companionship of old friends to help me be physically active and engaged. I feel my body. I honor it and what it needs, and I advocate for my own well-being.

LIVING WITH LONG-TERM ILLNESS

Wonderings

IF YOU HAVE BEEN affected by illness or low energy for a long time, do you feel helpless, overwhelmed, sad, lonely, and completely exhausted by this condition? Does it take all your strength and focus to deal with whatever the most important thing is (feeding a child, paying a bill, making that one phone call), and is there nothing left for the rest of your day? Are you tired of being sick, and do you need an immeasurable amount of self-compassion to make it through each day? Each time you gain a little strength, do you need to use it to mourn the losses that you are suddenly able to see? Does the world give people who are sick the message that they don't matter? Is it hard to find your grounding and to know the importance of your simple existence when society discounts your being and your contribution?

Affirmations

I AM ENOUGH. Simply by being, I have the right to take my place in the world. I matter and contribute, whatever my state of health, or strength, or whatever age I am. I have a solid relationship with my body, and I love every cell that gives me life. No matter how ambivalent I might sometimes feel about where my journey has taken me, I am grateful to be here, breathing. I acknowledge all of my cells for their daily struggle with energy, and I thank them for doing all that they can, every day, to support my well-being. Just for this moment, I find one place of just-rightness in my body—the pad of a finger, the crook of an elbow, an earlobe—here I can be myself and rest.

Theme 3

LONELINESS

AND COMMUNITY

ISOLATION AND LONELINESS

Wonderings

ARE YOU SOMETIMES so lonely that it cracks your bones and the marrow seeps out? Are you aching for intimacy, for warm curiosity, and for the give and take of rich conversation? Do you love connection and care and liveliness? Are there particular people you long to be with? Does their absence make you ache? Or does your missing stretch over your lifetime? Do you miss people you have never met, and an intimacy you've never had a chance to experience? Do you miss your friends, friends you have not yet found? Would you love to learn who you would be if you were happily held in a warm and joyful group that loved you?

Affirmations

TAP INTO my resilience when I feel alone. Even when my space is empty of company, I remember who I am. I nourish myself with a sense of all the people in the world. I feel their energy and know my own commonality with them. I give myself my memories of crowds, how people look, smell, and sound, and the richness of what it feels like to be together, even when we are apart. Although there are times when I am physically separated from my community, I am not separate.

TOO MANY PEOPLE
IN TOO LITTLE SPACE

Wonderings

ARE YOU LIVING too close to too many people at one time?
Are there so many people around you in so little room that
you would like to scream, except that you couldn't bear to add
anything to the noise and chaos that are already here? Or would
you just like to scream until you fully expressed the irritation
inside? Does the irritation rise when there is no separation or
distance? Do you ache for minutes or hours of aloneness when
there would be peace around you? But do you worry that these
people need you? Would you like to have a remote control that
would let you put everyone on pause until your nervous system
rediscovered its center? Do you need spaces of quiet, autonomy,
and choice? Would it be wonderful if others noticed your needs
and made room for them?

CLAIM A ZONE of peace for myself. No matter what is happening around me, I find my inner quiet. Inside of me, I hold onto silence and let it nourish me. It is a still place in my heart, and I can touch it even in the middle of chaos and noise. Just for this moment, I trust that all of the people here can manage their own lives, and I know that it is not just acceptable but necessary for me to breathe, and for me to care for myself with tenderness and acknowledgment.

NOSTALGIA FOR A STOPPED WORLD

Wonderings

DO YOU SOMETIMES miss the time when the world became very quiet? Was there a strange peacefulness in the silence of the stopped world? Did you enjoy the way the air smelled when no one was driving? Was there a merciful quality to the sudden cessation of social engagements? Did you have the chance to stay home instead of always being out or always traveling? Did you luxuriate in the expanses of unscheduled time? Are you sometimes afraid that you won't find that quiet again? Was the downtime an unprecedented and unexpected chance to catch your breath?

Affirmations

A **S THE WORLD** picks up speed after slowdowns and stoppages, I hold onto the pace that is right for me. I know my own rhythms. I know how quickly my brain likes to think and the speeds at which my body likes to move. I call on the knowledge of a very slow time to inform my choices and my understanding of what is healthy and good for me. Sometimes I am quicker than the world, and sometimes I move with more deliberation than the world does. I slow down when I want to, and I breathe as deeply as I need to breathe, no matter how quickly things around me are moving. My mind is sometimes a deep, slow, wide river, and sometimes a quick, burbling stream. I let the world go its own speed while I go my own speed. I clear space for myself. I breathe fully.

GUILT ABOUT
LOVING SOLITUDE

Wonderings

ARE YOU NOTICING how much the solitary life nourishes
you? Does the relative silence of solitude fill an ache in you that
you didn't even know you had? An ache for peace, for quiet, and
for timelessness? Are you sometimes afraid that you will turn
inward and never come out again? Do you need to know that you
still belong to the human race even when you love being alone?
Would you love to live in a world where your pleasure in solitude
didn't come at a cost? Would you love to have the capacity to
create space for yourself and to know that you were still flexible
and responsive and embedded in community?

HOLD THE PART of myself that loves solitude and doesn't want to engage with the larger world with compassion. I embrace my own rhythm and know that it does not have to come at the expense of others. I allow myself to simply want what I want. I celebrate the moments of pleasure and ease that are good for my body, even when they are different from what others want. I am complex. I see our interdependence and the ways in which pleasure and suffering are so interwoven in present-day life. I know that my feelings of happiness do not cause others' suffering and that I do not abandon those who are in pain when I feel relief. I know that I lighten the burden of the world when I feel joy, even when I preserve my beloved solitude. I celebrate solitude as a birthright of humanness.

WAITING FOR SOMEONE WHO DOESN'T COME

Wonderings

WHEN SOMEONE you are waiting for doesn't arrive on time, are you ambushed by a deep and devastating sense of aloneness? Do you worry that you made a mistake and came at the wrong time, or to the wrong place? Do you start to worry that something bad has happened, or that the person you are supposed to be meeting has fallen ill, or even died? Do you need information and clarity? Do you feel helpless, and sometimes are you afraid that you don't matter to the other person? As time goes on, do you start to worry that you've been abandoned? Has this happened to you before? Do you sometimes feel a shift into determination and having to rely fully on yourself for dependability and presence? Are you shocked at what can happen in a few seconds, and how it can impact your body for some time afterward?

Affirmations

ACCOMPANY MYSELF with love in the empty space. Even in the emptiness and not-knowing, I do not leave myself. I use warmth, affection, and acknowledgment to fill the spaces that are made empty by fear. Even when I make mistakes, and when other people make mistakes, are late, or do not come, I still love myself. I take my own fear of abandonment seriously and know that it comes from historical foundations. I call on creativity and self-care when I set up meetings with others. My mattering does not depend on others' punctuality and follow-through. I am never alone when I am with myself.

LEFTOVERS FROM
THE PANDEMIC

ARE YOU TIRED of staying away from people, but does it still feel like you should? If you were a mask wearer, do you have sudden moments of panic when you realize you are out without one? Are you bewildered and shocked by health crises and distance, and are you trying to figure out whether you still belong, and whether other people still belong to you? Or if you have never had a sense of belonging, does the distance confirm your sense that you don't belong? Would you enjoy contact and connection and belonging, especially if it could be good for everyone's health? Do you love warm interactions with people, but does your body still tense with closeness? Do you ache to be able to move into warmth no matter what the distance is and no matter what you and other people are doing for safety?

I AM GENTLE with myself when my need for safety stops me from having the closeness I would like. I am gentle with myself when my need for touch is greater than my need for safety. I respond with fluidity and when I want to, I release my fear, so that my body is not afraid of closeness or contact. I remember that our skin needs people, body heat, and touch. Even when I choose less contact, I am warm with myself and others. I am a responsive being, and I make choices based on clarity, love, and relationship with the present moment, rather than with the past.

Theme 4

WORK AND

CONTRIBUTION

WORK AND MONEY

Wonderings

DO YOU FEEL FRUSTRATED and helpless about the whole question of work and income? Do you long to have a passion that would lift you up and over all of the regular blocks and stoppages that are connected with the working life? Do you wish that you had something you loved to do, that people would pay you well for, that would be long-lasting and provide sustainability for you and the people you love? Are you worried about having work or income at all? Do you need work and income and a flow of at least sustainability, if not abundance? Would you like history and world events to cooperate with you and make earning and working easy? Would it be good to have a financially rewarding dream of your own?

I HAVE A GOOD PLACE in this world, and my gifts are meaningful. I work for others and for myself, supporting myself and the people who are dependent on me, without forgetting my gifts. I make space for creativity and dreaming. I am open to my dreams becoming clear, and I manifest my dreams in my own time, and I know that that time can be now. I value a world where everyone's gifts matter and are respected, and I value my resources, my gifts, and my contributions, as well as those of others. I love abundance and open space and responsiveness in my heart and in my life.

TOO MUCH WORK

Wonderings

ARE YOU BEING RUN so ragged that you barely have time to stop and breathe? Is it close to impossible to figure out how to schedule work and at the same time make sure there is space for self-care and for loved ones? Do you worry about the relentlessness of the pace of your work and the toll it is taking on your heart? Do you feel an immense gentleness for your body and gratitude for all the support it is giving you? Would you like to have the perfect balance of just enough work, the right income, and time to rest and enjoy life?

BRING MY FOCUS to my body and my heart, to support myself in my efforts to keep all the balls I am juggling in the air. I release myself from any unnecessary have-to's that leave me believing that I must juggle, and I invite myself to pick things up and put things down one at a time, with self-gentleness and care. I honor my breath and my attention for the self-care they support. I turn toward myself in this moment with kindness and presence, and I notice how my body responds to my warmth. I feel gratitude to my body for its contribution to me, and I make space for rest. I am resilient, and rest and gratitude feed my resilience.

MAKING MISTAKES

Wonderings

AFTER YOU HAVE made a mistake, even if no one else would think of it as a mistake, is the shame so strong internally that you can't even believe that you still belong? Do you find it very hard to look people in the face, and when they are kind and responsive, do you worry that they can't possibly mean it? Do you exclude yourself with your own conviction that you should disappear, even when others are not excluding you? Do you hate making mistakes so much that you stop breathing and turn both inward and away from yourself simultaneously? Is your longing for flawlessness so great that it is almost unbearable, at least for you?

FEEL UNCONDITIONAL WARMTH for myself. I understand that mistakes are necessary for learning, and I learn everything I can from my mistakes. I celebrate knowing that mistakes mean I am alive and willing to take the risks necessary for learning and growing. I belong to myself and the world, no matter how I perform. My belonging is irrevocable and is connected to my humanness, rather than to my function. I am gentle with my own self-contempt, my desire to turn away from myself, and with my own shame. I believe in my essential contribution and in the worth and power of my presence and my love. I am here as I am, and that is enough.

WHEN PEOPLE AREN'T CONTRIBUTING

Wonderings

ARE YOU TIRED of other people not pulling their weight? Are you bored with trying to fill in for what other people aren't doing? Is there irritation, disgust, and even fury about people not realizing that they are a weight in a system, a part of a community, and that if they don't work, other people have to make up for them? Is there any exhaustion from working alone? And when you aren't acknowledged for doing more than your share, is that even more of a weight on you? Would you love it if there were workplaces where this never happened and that you could work in one of them?

ACCOMPANY MYSELF with warmth and reassurance, especially when I am impacted by systemic and personal failures. When people aren't carrying out their responsibilities, I speak with them about the impact on me and others, and I make clear requests for change. I support myself to have clarity about where responsibility lies, and to communicate with the power structures about what is needed. Where power structures are nonresponsive or ineffective, I have faith in my own ability to be creative and persistent, and to advocate for myself, either by staying where I am, or by making a decision to leave.

WHEN PEOPLE ARE ALWAYS WORKING

Wonderings

WHEN SOMEONE on a team never stops working, do you despair for everyone's health and sanity? Do you worry about inhuman standards being set and about unrealistic expectations? Do you wish everyone understood the importance of breaks and time off from work for well-being and creativity? Do you wish for a shared value on work-life balance and for human life outside of work?

HOLD THE VALUE of people existing and mattering apart from their work life. I advocate for the importance of balance for both creativity and effectiveness. In the presence of others' workaholism, I allow myself to feel into my center and my rootedness. I feel my separateness from others' anxious bodies, and I work from my own calm and supported focus, taking the breaks I need and leaving work in the space I have created for it, fully enjoying myself as a nonworking being.

BURNOUT

Wonderings

SWEET BRAIN, are you fizzing and bubbling with everything that you are expected to produce? Are you up against a terrible, paralyzing ineffectiveness? Have you run out of neurotransmitters, and are you out of fuel? Do you need rest and fun and spontaneous play, and moments of shouting laughter or giggles or snorts or chortles to bring oxygen and a flood of warmth to your brain? Are you in need of intensive care? Do you need to be nourished and nurtured and fed with emotional warmth and sweetness? Preferably for years? Can you no longer work the way you used to? Do you need to find new ways of living that let you contribute and be sustainable, even when you are unable to pull the heavy loads that you were able to pull before?

CARE FOR MYSELF as I am, with my present-moment capacity. I notice and do what most supports me, including rest and the activities that rejuvenate me and recharge my energy. I feel tenderness for the parts of me that lived through the difficult times, and appreciation for myself for surviving. I honor myself for my efforts and my contributions, and I recognize myself as a line of being that stretches through from my earliest memories to the present moment. I am still myself, no matter what I have lived through. I still matter, even as I work to heal from everything that has gone before. In this moment, and in every moment, I am enough.

Theme 5

FAMILY

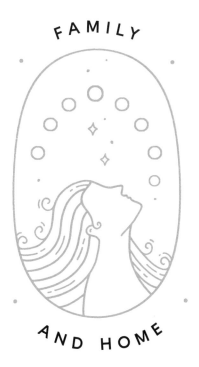

AND HOME

RESPONSIBILITY

Wonderings

ARE YOU FEELING overwhelmed with the constant calls for your attention? Do you have the sense of being a crisis call center for so many and at the same time needing to be able to focus on yourself in order to be able to pull things together, to make the money that needs to be made, and to take care of the things that need to be done? And at the same time, would you love to be kind and patient? Is patience an impossible dream right now? Is your nervous system hanging by its last thread? Would you like to feel comfortable asking for support from others to refrain from interrupting you when you are working? Do your nerves need a soothing balm of quiet in order to be able to focus and work?

Affirmations

I AM GENTLE and affectionate with myself, even when I am impatient. I acknowledge the tornness created by all the competing claims on my time and attention. I claim my own space to breathe, no matter what is happening around me. I have my own peace, my own quiet, and my own choice about how I think and how I feel. I am a breathing, existing being in my own right, and my sovereignty is inviolable. I understand the impossibility of doing it all, and I release myself from any internal pressure I have on myself to finish everything. I welcome my sense of humor about living in a state of constant triage.

GOOD PARENTING

Wonderings

ARE THERE SUDDEN MOMENTS of horror, a yawning sense of helplessness, bewilderment, or incapacity, when the world is asking you to do things as a parent that you don't know how to do, or that don't feel in integrity with your family's values? Are you stumped by things like improving your child's behavior, or homeschooling, or trying to decide about vaccinations, or returning to school? Are you torn between trying to take action, no matter how far beyond you that action seems, and total collapse and immobilization? Is it a stretch being a parent? Do you need to be gentle with yourself about how much you don't know? Is it hard to find authorities whose opinions you trust? Would you love it if you knew exactly what needed to be done, and how to do it, at all times?

I AM THE BEST PARENT for my child. My children don't want other parents—they want me. I don't need to be a different person. I simply need to move toward my warmest and most responsive way of being. As the world makes demands of my family, I listen to people whose opinions I trust, and make decisions that are flexible and responsive to the times. I take action and watch to see whether this action supports my child. If the answer is no, then I change my approach, even when it is hard for me. And all along the journey, I hold all of us with warmth and affection.

DOMESTIC CONFLICT

Wonderings

ARE THINGS SOMETIMES hard at home? And can it be hard and embarrassing to talk to anyone at all about what's happening? Do other people always have an opinion about what you should do? Are other people's opinions the opposite of helpful? Is there any need to name addiction, mental illness, or the aftereffects of trauma as a part of the picture? If you don't think about it when it's not happening, is it easier to survive? Do you feel shame when you think about the horror, overwhelm, and possibly the violence? Is there so much helplessness that it's easier just to hope that it will stop or get better on its own? Do you long for a sense of agency, so that you could take effective action that would help everyone and change the situation for the better?

KNOW THAT THINGS could be better for everyone, even when I don't know how to bring about change. I hold my resignation and surrender with warmth and tenderness, acknowledging historical impact and harm, and the consequences for everyone's nervous system, which take us toward collapse. No matter how much impact there has been for my nervous system, I remain alive to possibility, to hope, and I make movements toward transformation and healing, holding everyone involved as mattering. Even in difficult situations, I have capacity and agency. I take action for the greater good.

CARE FOR AGING PARENTS

Wonderings

ARE THERE SO MANY worries that come with making care decisions for aging parents? Has what used to be a relatively simple movement into assisted living become weighted with life-or-death overtones? Are your parents much more vulnerable than you wish they were, and much more in need of assistance than you can handle on your own? Do you love them, or honor them, and is there a terrible helplessness in not being able to do it all yourself? Do you long for the relief of being able to put them in a safe space, but now nothing is really safe? Do you need support, and do you wish it came with a guarantee of complete safety, so that everyone had the opportunity to finish their life journey with dignity and warm accompaniment?

Affirmations

AM DOING the best I can to support my parents. I love my parents and want the best possible care for them. When I put my parents in first place, I am no longer the main character in my own story, so I find ways to love them deeply and care for them responsibly, while remaining the center of my own life. I acknowledge the complexity of people's life paths and that I am unable to make everyone as safe as I would like them to be. I leverage my curiosity and my advocacy to change policies where necessary, and I lean into the best balance of care for others, along with self-care, so that I still have moments of freedom and joy, even as I am affected by the life journeys of the people I love. I stay open to what will support both my parents and myself.

FAMILY DISAGREEMENTS

Wonderings

WHEN YOU DISAGREE with a family member, do you go blank? Do you feel baffled and incredulous? Or do you turn into a prosecuting attorney and demolish the family member's argument? Is disagreement unbearable? Does your heart hurt from the bewilderment of two people who are so close seeing two different worlds? Are you tired of the discrepancy between visions? Do you long for shared reality? Do you worry that the difference in viewpoint will lead to exclusion, danger or the family or friendships falling apart? Is your heart tired and sad, either inside the collapse or inside the agitation? Do you sometimes feel disgusted or annoyed? Are you really, really wanting everyone, including yourself, to be capable of warm curiosity and respect?

Affirmations

SEE OUR DIFFERENT ways of looking at the world, and I follow the roots of each of our longings and our loves all the way back to the place where they meet. I see the divergence in the way we manifest our loves, and I fully mourn the divergence. I bow with respect for both of us. With affection and understanding, I accept my resistance to the way my family member sees the world.

SICKNESS AND DEATH

Wonderings

DO YOU FEEL so much grief and worry about the people that you love? Do you long to be able to protect them? Do you wish you could build a protective barrier between the world and everybody who has some vulnerability, whether you know them or not? Do you feel helplessness, tenderness, care, and fear? And is there a real heartfelt love for the world, along with the desire to keep the people you love alive and with you so that you will have them as long as possible? Do you love people, not just for them, but also for yourself?

ACKNOWLEDGE MY DEEP, deep love, my protectiveness, and my sorrow for every loss. I have warmth for my worry, and tenderness for my own helpless longings. I acknowledge the complexity in the way selfish love and unselfish love flow together. I take whatever action I can to make people I love safe, and I fully mourn the people I cannot protect.

Theme 6

MOURNING

OUR LOSSES

MISSING THE PEOPLE WITHOUT NAMES

Wonderings

AFTER BIG SOCIAL CHANGES, do you sometimes notice that you are missing the nameless people you saw regularly before everything changed? Do you miss the sweet interactions with the grocery store clerk or the mail carrier or the random person pumping gas next to you? Do you love being able to stand in line and shuffle along with a group of humans you don't know? Do you love being with people in space, reading their bodies, decoding what's happening, making jokes, and noticing others' emotions? Is it good to remember that our human bodies are social animals, that we have skin sensors devoted exclusively to detecting body warmth from other beings? And to remember that we have areas in our brains that tell us we're hungry for people, just as we have brain areas that tell us we're hungry for food?

WHEN I MISS PEOPLE, I mourn. I make sure not to skip the mourning. I notice the body pain in wanting to be with people, and I wrap myself in warmth, and I say to myself, "Of course you miss them, and even though you don't know their names, your missing is important." I nourish myself with memories of warm interactions. I feel tenderness for my grumpiness about change. I have affection for my own reaches toward connection, and I enjoy new connections. I trust that new connections will form, and are forming, whatever shape the world takes.

 FRIENDS

Wonderings

WHEN YOU ARE SEPARATED from your friends, are you like a pool that has lost its inflow of spring water, and can you feel yourself evaporating and becoming dry? Do you sometimes wonder what it would be like to live a life where you could keep everyone with you? Where people didn't disappear or move away or get lost or die? Do your eyes ache with a pining for the missing ones? And when you do reach out for one of the missing and your hand closes around smoke and more disappearance, is there a kind of devastation? Are you supporting yourself to feel the sadness today, and to be able to simply say, "I miss that person," instead of promising yourself to never make friends again?

EMBRACE THE POWER of my own love. The intensity of my heart and its love for people doesn't frighten me. I love and miss people from last week, and I love and miss people from past decades. I mourn the people who have been lost to time or geography or death. The memories that come about each person are welcome. They flow through me, and I do not get lost in them. I remember the love that others have had for me and I let it comfort me. I reach out to past people, living and dead, whenever it feels right, while locating myself firmly in present time. I am alive to new connections that my heart makes. I enjoy myself as a loving, connecting being.

ADVENTURE AND TRAVEL

Wonderings

WHEN YOU ARE NOT able to travel, or you choose not to travel in order to protect the world's ecosystems, do you feel stranded and bereft at home? Is there a relief that comes from driving or flying away from all your daily responsibilities? Does not traveling mean losing a stream of nourishment and engagement in the world? Do you miss the expansiveness of being in different places with different smells, flavors, new signs, different businesses, sidewalks, shops, road markings, leaves, fruits, clothing, humidity, and people speaking languages that aren't yours? In the slog of daily life, do you reward yourself with plans for future adventures? And when you are not able to make travel plans, is the lift of anticipation missing from life? Do you wish there were ways to be in safe and nonharmful contact with all of the different flavors that this planet has to offer?

PARTICIPATE FULLY in the life of this world. This is my planet, and I belong here, and it belongs to me. When I pick up a handful of rich, living soil, I'm touching nearly one million organisms. I glory in life as it comes to me. I enjoy walks as adventures and revelations. I explore adventures that are available and aligned with my integrity. My stewardship of nature and culture nourishes me, and the entire planet is mine to steward and contribute to, no matter where I am physically. I celebrate and give expression to my love of this world.

INTIMACY

Wonderings

ARE YOU FLAT-OUT lonely for intimacy? Are you gasping for a sense of closeness, of the joy of being known, of being most important, of having shared language, shared memories, and shared reality? Would you like to be with someone who could finish your sentences once in a while, and get the endings right? Do you love deep conversations that last for weeks? Would you love to know what someone else's favorite things were, and have yours known, too? Do you love intimacy with individuals, and intimacy with groups? Would you love it if the people giving you gifts knew you well enough that the gifts would land as wondrous mysteries that nourished you?

Affirmations

MOURN SEPARATION from others. At
the same time, I am deeply nourished by
my own company. I have affection for and
a sense of humor about who I am and what I love. I stay
with myself no matter what. I stop leaving myself behind.
I relinquish the hope that if I don't take care of myself,
others will notice and come to take care of me. While I care
for myself, I am also open to love and intimacy from others.
I take great pleasure in intimacy wherever it happens,
whether I'm on my own or in company, and I celebrate
depth and mutual understanding.

OPPORTUNITIES FOR GROWTH

Wonderings

HAVE YOU ALWAYS intended to start a growth practice such as meditation, journaling, playing a musical instrument, learning a foreign language, or taking up yoga? When you think about those old longings, and the lost time, and how well you would do these things if you'd started long ago, and how little time is left now, are you suffused with longing and regret? Are you angry at your younger self for your choices, and wishing for a big do-over for your life? Would you love to experience what your life would have been if you had had more resources, energy, and agency all along?

MOURN THE WAYS that a lack of support left me without the energy to learn and study. As I look back at my life with clear eyes, I see the ways in which I was not nourished, and I see my strengths. I celebrate my survival, and I enjoy myself as I am. With the clear vision of my own lifelong flow of resources comes self-forgiveness. There is no "too late." No matter my age, I let my passions inform my movements. I begin any pursuit that inspires me, without limiting myself. If I always wanted to play the cello, I begin playing the cello. If I always wanted to learn Japanese, I start studying Japanese. This is my life, and I make my own choices about what to do with it.

THOSE WHO HAVE DIED

Wonderings

ARE YOU STRIPPED of everything by the death of someone you love, like a piece of driftwood tossed out of the ocean? Is it difficult to recommit to life without this person? Does death sometimes call you? Do you search for this person wherever you go, as if your body doesn't understand death, and just thinks that you've lost your someone, and that if you look hard enough, you will find this person again? Are you crumpled and collapsed, and out of energy? Are you trying to keep living with only half of yourself here to work with? Is it hard to make food, listen to music, and do what has to be done? Do you need more time, more days, weeks, years with this person, so that everything could ripen and pass in its own time, until a time when you would really be ready to say good-bye?

CARRY MY BELOVED people with me for whatever amount of time I still need them. I say my different good-byes to each person who has died. I say them at the right time for me, no matter when the death occurred. I have an enormous gentleness for myself in my own dance with others' death: my resistances, my protests, and my gradual acceptance. At the same time that I acknowledge death, I am alive. Life is calling me, and I listen to its call. I taste flavors. I smell the sea and the earth and the car exhaust and the trees. I see all the greens of all the leaves. I feel what brick feels like, and stone, and grass, and cloth, and others' skin. My energy for life returns, and I welcome it. I release my loyalties to the dead and I know I will join them in my own good time.

Theme 7

LOVING

THE PLANET

THE CLIMATE CRISIS

Wonderings

IS THIS ISSUE BIGGER and more horrifying than human brains can easily hold? Are you struggling with a spotty capacity to understand the enormity of the climate crisis? Does your brain say, "La-la-la," and then suddenly swing to a vision of horror? And then is that unbearable, so you say "La-la-la" again? Do you blink back and forth between incomprehension and terrible worry and grief? Is nihilism an easier place to rest than the vastness of your sorrow? Do you need to be able to love yourself even when you are incapable of seeing, even when you rest in denial or nihilism? And does your capacity for compassion for all humans, and for our stunningly beautiful and beleaguered global ecosystem, blink in and out as well?

Affirmations

HAVE INFINITE WARMTH for myself as I work to understand the incomprehensible magnitude of the climate crisis, and I have great tenderness for my own moments of rest, when I close my eyes to all of it. With each new level of settled understanding that I gain, I integrate my new knowledge into my commitment and my responsiveness. I release the contracts I have to save the world all by myself, so that I can be an effective member of communities and collectives that are working for the kinds of change that seem important to me. I relinquish my helplessness. I join my strength with that of every other person in this world who loves this planet's ecosystems and is working for something better.

LOSING OUR
PLANETARY HOME

Wonderings

DO YOU FEEL a fatal homesickness for ecosystems that are gone or disappearing? Are the shame and inconsolable grief very close to the surface? Do they sometimes burst through into helpless rage or tears? Is there a line of exhaustion that runs down from your forehead and sinuses into your throat, chest, and belly? Is there not quite enough energy to complete anything, because every plan that leads into the future ends up in sorrow? Are you pulled back in time with a helpless grief for what is long gone and can never be regained? Do you try to direct your attention so you can shut out the sorrow? To not think about the dying birch trees, and what spring smelled like, or snow piled up so high you could jump off the roof and land softly in the heaps? Do you tell yourself, "Just don't remember, just don't remember"?

MY BODY and the planet's body are indivisible. My love for the particular places I have called home is powerful, and it matters, and my love will not kill me, even if the places disappear or are changed. I accompany myself in my mourning so that it continues to move and does not immobilize me. I notice the changes that the ecosystems are undergoing, and I notice the disappearing species and each breath of unique beauty that we are losing. I put my shoulder to the collective wheel for rescue and preservation in every way that is available to me.

THE ECOSYSTEMS

Wonderings

ARE YOU NOTICING a fatigue that lines your bones about the loss of the world's ecosystems? Is it impossible to grieve for each animal, plant, insect, bird, and person, for each being's home, lost in the fires and the droughts and the floods? And is there weariness from the helplessness, from the systemic nature of what is happening, from the continual stream of thoughts that are trying to find a way to change everything, to change anything, to change humans, to transform their brains, and to share reverence for each ecosystem, each plant, each phyto- and zooplankton? Is there fatigue from working to manage the screaming terror of loss? Do you love this planet's life forms more than can be borne when so much is going extinct? Do you long for shared reverence and a capacity to see that is so deeply rooted that it awakens everyone and changes everything?

INTEGRATE MY LOVE for the planet's ecosystems, my mourning, and my everyday life together in this body. These are all things I feel, and I bring them together simultaneously, rather than having to break them into pieces to survive them. My sadness makes sense. My worry makes sense. I make sense, in my complex patchwork of responsiveness, helplessness, immobilization, and action. I have agency, choice, leverage, power, and a voice, and I use them in ways that sustain me and energize me with meaning, purpose, and hope, as part of larger communities of mobilization in the service of my love for this planet.

THE BUMBLEBEES

Wonderings

DO YOU LOVE bumblebees and honeybees? Do the heavy, thick, fuzzy bodies of bumblebees give you the sense of direct connection to the earth? Is it unbearable when your yard is silent, and when the bees are not on the clover or the dandelions? Does it hurt to remember how much you love them? Does your tenderness and incredulity crush you? Do you wish you could hold onto your innocence? Do you wish that your love could protect the world's ecosystems? Are you stunned by the lack of shared reality with decision makers who are prioritizing money over the precious, irreplaceable ecosystems of the earth? Would you like to live in a world where it was impossible for humans not to perceive and care about consequences? Would you prefer it if humans had evolved more in the direction of preservation of life, and depth, and breadth of vision?

Affirmations

HAVE COMPANY in my love for the bumblebees of this planet. My worry and care are shared. I am part of a large community of worried people. We understand the serious threat of this time together. The more I am allied with fellow carers, the more powerful I am. My body knows that there is great togetherness in this love. Standing in the togetherness, I live with my own grief without collapse and remain able to take action.

INDESTRUCTIBLE NATURE

Wonderings

DO YOU MISS a past when the world and nature seemed inexhaustible and resilient? Do you mourn the passing of a time when the oceans and forests teemed with life? When the water, air, and the natural environment felt relatively safe? Did you love the sense of abundance, adventure, exploration, and wonder? Do you worry about how climate change will affect the future, including the future of not only the oceans, trees, plants, animals, birds, and insects, but also the future of all the children and grandchildren in the world? Do you worry about how the people you love will be able to make their way in a changed world?

FEEL EXQUISITE GENTLENESS for my own mourning. I acknowledge a sadness so huge that it fills the atmosphere. I support my cells in their longing for an inexhaustibly abundant planet. I feel compassion for our beloved planet and for everyone's and everything's future. I tap into the shared grief of the millions of people who worry with me, so that I am not feeling the weight of all this on my own. I love our tenderness for the fragility of our ecosystems. My mourning supports the growth of my engagement and participation, just as a trellis supports the growth of flowering roses.

WORLD PEACE

Wonderings

DO YOU WORRY about the effect of scarcity on world peace? Is your worry a constant background hum? Do you fear the effect of the climate crisis, lost land, relentless heat, drought, famine, and migration on everyone's ability to work together and solve problems? Do you ache for a longer period of ecosystem resilience, so that humans could have a chance to straighten themselves out and make decisions that would lead to world abundance, to homes for everyone, to unprecedented creativity and generosity, to every voice finally mattering? Are you longing for the peace that comes when all are taken care of? The relaxing of the body and mind that happens with trust that every voice matters and that conflicts will be attended to with care and skill, in a world that sees its own abundance?

NO MATTER WHAT is happening in the larger world, the world I create is calm, generous, and responsive. I feel warmth for my enormous worry and I stand beside myself to comfort myself and acknowledge the scale of the problems that lie ahead of us. When my capacity to imagine a good future flickers and the despair is too much for me, I let myself rest from imagining at all, and I stay rooted in a present-time good moment. I notice the love and laughter that are abundant, and I accept the territory of the world that I can affect with good humor and humility. I do not blame myself for incapacity to change the trajectory of history. I contribute where I can, on whatever scale is doable for me.

Theme 8

EMOTIONS

AND LONGINGS

FEAR

Wonderings

ARE YOU ALWAYS AFRAID? Does the world seem dangerous? Is there always something scary around corners and behind doors? Would you like a little acknowledgment that you have very good historical reasons to consider the world threatening? Is it hard to breathe fully, and is it hard to digest your food? Do you shake sometimes? And are your hands weaker than you want them to be? Did your nervous system go into hypervigilance decades ago and never come out? Would you need a century of predictable peace and safety for your body to finally relax?

Affirmations

EVEN THOUGH I have been frightened in the past, in this moment, in this breath, reading this book, I am safe. I acknowledge my past, and I step through time and space to the part of me that is still lost. I freeze the danger and I name the fear, the aloneness, the helplessness, and the sorrow. If things are not safe in my present-time life, I feel my own strength, and I make a safe place for myself in my heart, in my inviolable center. Whenever my found-self becomes willing, I bring my found-self home with me, to have a good and safe place in my heart, whatever is happening in the outer world. I breathe deeply. My body relaxes at its own speed.

ANGER

Wonderings

ARE YOU SOMETIMES so angry or do you feel so threatened that the rage boils out of you? Does it scald everything it touches, and do you feel helpless to stop it? Is it too big for your body? Does it overtake you and leave you not even recognizing yourself? And does it temporarily give you power and then leave you ashamed and alone? Is there a helplessness in you as you feel it rise? Did you give up trying to change it long ago? Do you worry about it harming the people who depend on you? Do you try to find a way to live with it by fatalistically accepting it as a part of yourself? Is there a terrible resignation? Would you love to have a way to both integrate it as life force and have it do no harm?

AM ANGRY because I love. My life force is powerful, and unified with love, it is protective and fiercely compassionate. When anger arises, it points to things I care about. My anger makes sense, and I trust and value it. When I am angry at people, I follow the trail of their actions and words to discover what I love. From that clear opening of love, I can take action to protect and care for whatever may have felt threatened. I receive feedback willingly and integrate information about what works. When I am angry at systems, I let my anger and my rage and my love work togther to fuel my ongoing, sustained actions on behalf of justice. From this place, I can live my commitment to nonviolence. I am simultaneously angry and fiercely compassionate. I know myself in my anger, and I know what I care about.

GRIEF

Wonderings

WHEN GRIEF RISES, does it carry you away? Are you overwhelmed by sorrow, and do you try to think of something else, or do something else? Do you hope people don't realize that those are tears leaking out of your eyes? Are you yourself confused by the volume of grief, wondering how this could belong to just you? Do you wonder if you are crying for the world, every minute of every day? Are even your dreams sad? Do you have the sense that no one else should know about this grief, because it would be too heavy for them? Do you try to keep it to yourself in order to keep the people you love safe from it? Would Earth need to become a full water planet without land to have enough space for all the tears you would cry if you ever actually started to grieve?

EVEN WHEN I TOUCH grief that is bigger than I can hold, I'm still here. I feel my body and I know myself. The truth of grief rejuvenates me and is a part of my nuanced experience of being alive. For this moment, even when I am surrounded by loss, I am not lost. I feel my grief, and I feel all of my other feelings, too. I release all my contracts to carry the grief of the world, acknowledging that that is too much for any one human, and I am only one human. I reach into the earth with my emotional roots and nourish myself with what the trees and the rivers know about loss. I am willing to be accompanied in my grief by other humans, other beings, and by nature itself.

DISGUST AND CONTEMPT

Wonderings

DO YOU HAVE serious reservations about humanity's capacity for goodness, intelligence, and solid decision making? Is there a sneering judgment that hovers behind your facial expression much of the time? Would you like to do one huge eye roll to show how you feel about people's behavior? Are you repulsed by the news, and exhausted by the unfolding of events? And at the same time that you feel contempt and disgust for others, do you also feel these emotions toward yourself for being so judgmental? Would you like to feel your own condemnation lift, so that you could enjoy some hope and optimism for a change?

Affirmations

I **HAVE WARMTH** and a sense of humor about my own inclination to judge. I turn toward my contemptuous self with affection. I feel the beating heart of my love and fear for humanity inside my contempt and disgust. I collect all the broken pieces of my heart and bring them back together, and I feel my heart whole again. I release all my contracts that block hope in order to save myself from disappointment. Even when I cannot hope, I welcome the possibility, remembering that some say that hope is not really hope until all basis for hope is gone. I step into the paradox of realism and delight. I feel not only contempt but also the full range of emotions—grief, delight, fear, anger, joy, shame, disgust, and awe—the dimensions of life that give it color and vibrancy.

DESIRES AND LONGINGS

Wonderings

ARE YOU FILLED with desires and longings that ache for something, but you don't know what? Does it feel like, if you could just figure out what you want and get it, then something within you would relax? Is it almost painful to want so much, but not to know how to aim your intention? Is it like having an invisible sliver in your foot, so that every step is a discomfort? And sometimes do you know what you want, but it's out of reach, and is that unbearable? Are you unsure of how to ever be calm or settled if you can't know what you want, or get what you want? Do you wish there were someone in the world who knew you so well that they could tell you what you want, and how to get what you want?

Affirmations

FEEL MY ALIVENESS. I understand my own longings, even when they have no target. My undirected longings are for direct contact with life itself, in a form that makes sense to my body. They are the language of my love for this life. I enjoy myself as a being with desires, and I am open to many strategies for fulfillment. When there are things I want that aren't available to me, I celebrate the strength of my desire, I read my love from the form of my longings, and I release whatever I am longing for to the universe, keeping my love with me.

PERFECTIONISM AND SHAME

Wonderings

DO YOU WANT EVERYTHING you do to be just right? Would it make you bulletproof, to have nothing be wrong, ever? When things are not quite right, is it excruciating? Is there a part of you that lives with relentless, exhausting shame about the state of things, and about what you are able to do? Are you compelled to keep planning and replanning without stopping to try to make things perfect? Is the desire for perfection a merciless drive inside you that has no idea what it is to be human? And so do you sometimes try not to do anything at all, so that you can avoid the hell of relentless shame?

I AM HUMAN. It's not my job to be perfect. Rather than intending to do things without any errors, I do things so that they meet needs, and I do the things I do with warmth. Sometimes I prioritize beauty. Sometimes timeliness. Sometimes functionality. Sometimes meaning. I shift from a static, dualistic world of perfect/imperfect to a world of ever-flowing divinely human needs. Even though I long for invulnerability from shame, I relinquish any agreements I have with myself to strive for perfection. Instead of dismissing my accomplishments for not meeting my inhuman standards, I appreciate and enjoy the things I do. I celebrate the flow of my life energy. I respect and appreciate my willingness to risk imperfection or failure, honoring the courage it takes to engage with life. I have a sense of humor about my own humanness, and I take satisfaction and joy from my human life.

Theme 9

LIVING THE

CREATIVE LIFE

WRITER'S OR CREATIVE BLOCK

Wonderings

ARE YOUR FEET STUCK in mud when you try to move forward on your project? Do all the ideas that crowd into your mind when you are free suddenly disappear when you try to work? Do you dread the peculiar blankness that comes up? Is everything else easier to do, from housework to email? And once you get your mind to start working, is every creative act— every line, every note, every word—a direct highway to shame hell? Is nothing ever what you want it to be? Do you spend days in relationship with the blank page with nothing to show for it? Do you feel sorrow, shame, and bewilderment about the lost time? Would you love for a direct flow of energy from the part of you that wants to create to the part of you that does the creative work?

Affirmations

TRUST THAT my blocks are part of a larger cycle of creating and pausing. I accept myself and this pattern. Remembering that there are in-breaths and out-breaths to the creative process, I see the patterns behind my creative blocks and I feel warmth for them. I hear the love and care that are hidden behind my hesitations. In my blocks, I find my sense of the value of beauty and grace, of mattering and meaning. The way I reflect the world is unique, and it captures nuances that others do not see. I have affection for my wish for my work to be world shattering and to contribute to humanity, and I have a gentle sense of humor about my longings. My voice matters. My vision matters. I work at the times and pace that are best for me, and I give myself breaks for self-care.

DEADLINES

Wonderings

ARE YOU OVERWHELMED by urgency and deadlines? Do you need a year of space to work on this project, or at least a month, instead of only having the time until the deadline? Do you feel like a distractible cat in a world full of moving feathers? Is it extremely hard to settle? Are you surprised when you get a small piece done, and then are you dismayed because so many more sentences are needed? Is it almost impossible to stay focused? Do you long for a dry clarity and a sharp mind to cut through your own dissociation and distractibility so that you can snap all this out and feel the powerful satisfaction of being on target and on time? Would you like to be able to be affectionate with your own incapacity, to bring yourself warmth like a beautiful embroidered crazy quilt spread over everything?

Affirmations

ACKNOWLEDGE MY ANXIETY with care, so that my body has a sense that I know myself and am receiving my own messages. When deadlines bother me, I acknowledge my own love of freedom, spontaneity, and emergence. I see myself as part of a larger effort and know that my contribution is a piece of the whole, and that meeting my own deadlines helps everyone else. I feel a sense of being with others in our shared purpose, and this awareness gives me a sense of accompaniment and mutual support. I ground myself in what I can do in this moment, while holding the intention for timely completion. I know what needs to be done, and I know how to do it. I am exactly right for the task as it develops, in the time that I have.

MISSING COLLABORATION

Wonderings

DO YOU GET TIRED, working all alone? Do you feel lonely and bored, and do you sometimes need to use substances and behaviors to keep yourself on track on your own? Do you long for give and take, for the mutual sparking of creativity? Do you miss teamwork? Does it go against the grain to be working without creative input from others? Is there something about creating together that feels most right? Would your ideal work team be gathered in one room, with jokes, stories, and laughter? Do you wish to be inspired by others and to share the load of creativity and production?

EVEN WHEN I AM physically alone and don't want to be, I carry my cocreators, living and dead, real and imagined, with me. I take creative sparks from what I read, from what I see, from the small interactions of daily life. I welcome the different parts of myself and the sense of creative collaboration from the inside out. I recognize that companionship is available, in human and nonhuman form, from the present and past and future, and I invite all forms of accompaniment and cocreation, whatever my external circumstances.

CREATION SHAME

Wonderings

DO YOU ANTICIPATE negative judgments of your work? With every brushstroke, every word, every note, do you imagine that people will condemn and reject you? Do you expect people's bodies to turn away from you? In order to create, do you have to break through your own shame prohibitions, every step of the way? When you try to move toward your own creativity, do you sometimes have to push through an atmosphere of slime? Does the shame coat every cell of your being? Would you love to experience what it's like to create with a sense of being fully supported and encouraged? Would you love it if you could know that your work would be welcome?

MY **EXPRESSIONS** have their own audience, and my audience needs my expressions. My existence is necessary, and I contribute in ways that I know, and in ways that I don't know. While some bodies turn away from me, some turn toward me, and that is where mutual nourishment happens. I create from a place free of shame, in the spirit of expression, exploration, discovery, and meaning. The universe supports, encourages, and welcomes my creativity.

SOCIAL MEDIA DISTRACTION

Wonderings

DO YOU FIND YOURSELF continually refreshing pages for email or information, rather than doing your creative work? Is clicking so much easier than working? Does the fresh information that appears give you a sense of being able to accomplish something, or help you predict the world and feel safer? Are you sometimes desperate for news or understanding? When you are, might the next thing that comes up on the screen save you? Is the desire to keep checking a compulsion? Even when you tell yourself you will focus, do you still feel drawn to check email or social media, and do you feel helpless to resist that pull, as a piece of metal is drawn to a magnet? Instead of being magnetized by distraction, would you love to have a capacity for deep focus that would magnetize your attention on what you want to be working on?

Affirmations

STEP OFF the hamster wheel of continual checking. I am calm and self-connected. I replenish myself with flexibility, responsiveness, and freedom, supporting my body, my mind, and my immune system. I focus on my work with ease, and distractions float past me like soap bubbles, without claiming my attention. I gently steer my attention with my intention. I know what I want to create, and my message flows out of me in my own way. I feel centered and free to consciously choose where to focus, and I focus on that which will give me energy, meaning, and progress on my goals.

CREATING SOMETHING YOU LOVE

Wonderings

HAVE YOU CREATED something wonderful? Are you totally excited and buoyed up with anticipation about sharing this creation? Would you enjoy appreciation for how much satisfaction and exhilaration this creation has sparked and for how gorgeous it is for you? Do you appreciate yourself for having brought it into the world? Do you love the way that this material evolves into completely new explorations whenever you touch it? Is the creativity it fosters a little like holding a flower that is unfolding in your hands? And does this creation hold the complexity you love? Are you filled with a delight that spreads up through your chest and even hurts a little bit as it pushes through your shoulders? Does your back crack as you expand with breath to hold the joy? In this moment, are you so grateful to be alive?

CELEBRATE MY CREATION. Delight at its emergence fills me. I feel satisfaction, both that my creation has emerged and been completed, and that it came from me. I release any contracts I have not to appreciate myself. I step outside of my culture of no-celebration and invite full-bodied enjoyment that fills every cell. Satisfaction is the nourishment of artists—satisfaction, some rest, and the dream of the next creation.

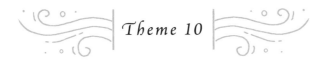

Theme 10

CARING FOR

OUR ENERGY

BOREDOM AND MEANING

Wonderings

HAS COLOR GONE OUT of the world? Are things gray and empty? Does everything run together, without edges? Are you more bored than you can endure? Do you remember waking up in the mornings when you were a child and wanting to jump out of bed to get to your day, and do you wonder where that energy has gone? Do you have to force yourself to move through your tasks now? And is there little that lifts your heart with joy? Do you ache for a sense of variety, adventure, contribution, and meaning? Do you want the easy movement and flow that come with engagement?

Affirmations

ACKNOWLEDGE THE WEIGHT that comes when my life energy is not engaged. I wrap myself in affection even when I don't see any color in the world. Despite the temptation to blame myself for this state of affairs, I see my life and my burdens with clarity and self-compassion. I remember my joyful self, and I remember the moments when I lost my joy. I visit each moment in turn, collecting the parts of myself that I have abandoned to shock, lost trust, fear, shame, rage, and alarmed aloneness. Whatever my beliefs about resources, I open to and receive support from sources that are beyond myself—ancestors, nature, spirit, friends, or beloved animals. I am willing to be loved by humans, and I am willing to be moved by what life wants from me.

DEEP FATIGUE

Wonderings

ARE YOU TIRED all the time? Does the weariness steal your energy and make your bones ache? Does it infiltrate your joints and run through your blood vessels, sapping your oxygen? Are your cells unsure where to find fuel? Does sleep give you little beyond a brief period of unconsciousness? Do you add to your exhaustion with self-contempt and anger at yourself? Is there a sea of shame to swim through in addition to the tiredness? Does every action come at a cost? And do you have to count up all the actions you need to do and make plans to get through each day, deciding what is most important to spend energy on? Do you try to prioritize the living beings who depend on you? Do you wish for every kind of abundance, most particularly abundance of energy?

Affirmations

HAVE ENOUGH ENERGY for this moment. I honor my mitochondria, the engines of my cells. No matter how fatigued I am, I bow to my cells and make myself available for them to contribute to me. I am exquisitely gentle with my tired self, celebrating my small movements and taking great care with my supplies of energy. I am willing to ask for and receive help and support. I explore whatever avenues for healing are accessible to me, and I am creative with and responsive to what comes toward me.

THE COST OF ADDICTION

Wonderings

SOMETIMES, DOES ALL your brain energy go to trying to figure out when you will be able to access your addictive substance or behavior? Do you only have peace, and does the craving only stop, when you can access it? Do you spend most of your time thinking about it? Does your addiction help you do what you need to do? Is there something about this substance or behavior that makes life livable? Does life feel unlivable much of the time? Does your addiction make up for difficulties with both meaning and energy? Do you worry about the cost of your addiction, not just to you and your health, but to all your relationships? Would you love to live in a world where the imbalances that drive us into compulsive actions would all be balanced, where your body would feel good most of the time, and life would be livable?

 **HAVE GREAT GENTLENESS** for myself in the way my brain responds to my addiction. For this moment, this hour, this day, I value my sobriety. I am supported and balanced by resources greater than myself and my addiction. I call on nature, ancestors, love, community, and on support. I acknowledge each way my addiction tries to take care of me, and I see the costs that it exacts with clarity and self-compassion. I release my addiction from each contract it has with me, even when I have hundreds of contracts. I hold onto my faith in myself and in my ability to lean into whatever is greater than me that sustains me.

BEING UNABLE TO SLEEP

Wonderings

DO YOU WONDER if long, restful sleep will ever find you again? Do you worry that you have forgotten how to sleep? Do you wake at 2 a.m. and then toss and turn, unable to turn your mind or your physical anxiety off? When you wake up in the early hours, do you feel dread, waiting for the never-ending merry-go-round of worries and resentments? And then during the days, do you drag yourself from task to task in an exhausted state? Are you bewildered that humans could be made this way, with a dark-of-night flaw that can wake them up, make it hard to get back to sleep, and knock people off balance? Would you like to be remade, so that easy, restful sleep was one of your superpowers?

Affirmations

EVEN WHEN I WAKE in the early hours, I am gentle and warm with myself. I wrap my brain snugly with acknowledgment and affection, so that it can feel itself being held. I say thank you to each anxious thought, to each turn of the merry-go-round: "Thank you for working so hard to take care of me." "Thank you for trying to anticipate the difficulties." I breathe deeply, nourishing myself with the knowledge that deep breathing and mindfulness also restore the brain. During the days, when I am tired and wish I had slept, I am kind to my tired self. I experiment with things that can support good sleep, allowing myself to try new strategies, even things that scare me, like sleep hygiene and stopping all screen time before sleep. I refine and celebrate the art of napping whenever possible. And through it all, I accompany myself with love.

WORRYING AND ENERGY

Wonderings

DO YOU FEEL your life energy trickling away from you as you worry? Do your worries sap your strength and take you away from yourself? Does your worry jangle your nerves and make your chest buzz? Does it make it hard to rest? Does your mind never stop? Do the thoughts run repetitively, without ceasing, and do they keep you out of the present moment? Is it hard to tell if you are more afraid or more lonely? Is it hard to find yourself within the static so that you can know yourself and relax? Do you wish inner peace were a real, lived experience? Do you long to be able to use all your capacities to build and nourish your life, rather than expending them on anxiety?

EVEN WHEN I WORRY, I find my way back to my own center. No matter how much anxiety there is, I can find my peaceful self. I am rooted in the earth, and I pull the calm and the quiet out of the ground into my belly, and bring peace to my heart and my lungs. I let my mind pause, using my focus on my breath to support a mind full of self-warmth, run by life rather than by thoughts. I know that I often feel both fear and alarmed aloneness, and I commit to caring for and providing companionship for the parts of myself that feel scared or alarmed and alone. I let them know that they will have someone, somewhere to offer warmth and witness to them. I offer myself this accompaniment fully and generously; I nourish myself with love, no matter where my emotions wander.

SOCIAL MEDIA'S EFFECTS

Wonderings

DO YOU WORRY about the effect of the modern world? Do you watch people with their devices, absorbed separately, no one talking with each other? If you remember a time before devices, do you feel shocked, horrified, angry, and hopeless? Do you miss the time before smartphones? Do you wonder whether we'll lose each other in technology? Do you wish for moments when all the Wi-Fi and social media networks would go down safely, without anyone panicking, and people would just talk to each other and laugh together? If devices have been around as long as you can remember, is there acceptance of technology and bewilderment about the upset some people feel about it? No matter when you grew up, do you love to see and be involved in fully engaged conversations, and are you sometimes grateful for the opportunities technology can give us to have these conversations anytime, anywhere?

Affirmations

MOURN THE LOSSES of the modern world, and I celebrate the new connections that are possible. I mourn and release the past, and step into the present. Where necessary, I let myself have sadness about any local connections that have faded. At the same time, I'm open to making friends of all ages with the people I see in my neighborhood or around my work. I also embrace the global friendships and partnerships that are emerging. I commit myself fully to my conversations, however they take place. I am completely alive to all possible communication, and I delight in my friends and relatives.

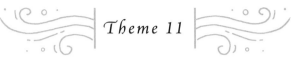

Theme 11

HELPLESSNESS

AND CHOICE

WANTING
CHOICE

Wonderings

WOULD YOU LIKE to have every kind of choice? Would you like to have all the choices that come with abundance? How to spend money, what to do with your time, how involved to be with people, what to use your brain energy on, and what emotions you are feeling? When you don't have abundance and choice, do you sometimes have a sense of restriction or claustrophobia? Or even sometimes of frustration, anger, and rage? Do you feel helpless and worried about larger systems that steal people's choice: systemic racism, systems of economics, politics, gender, or religion? Would you love to experience a world that was thoughtfully abundant, with care taken for ecosystems, all the species of the earth, with everyone mattering, and full of choice for everyone?

EXPLORE THE PLACES where I stop myself from exercising choice. I release the agreements I have with myself to react with anger when choice is limited. I move toward choice. I choose my path. Each of my steps belongs to me. In the places where I resent a lack of abundance, I claim my inner expansiveness, generosity, and sense of possibility. I acknowledge and mourn the impact of larger systems on myself and the people I love. I take the actions that are mine to take. I choose with an eye to joy, contribution, and satisfaction.

PUBLIC POLICIES

DO YOU FEEL BEWILDERED and helpless about the decisions that government and leadership make? Are you stunned or shocked, and do you sometimes suddenly realize that you are angry and even sad about public policies? Do you wish you lived in a country where you had shared reality with the government of that country? Do you doubt that is even possible? Are you tired to death of decisions being made that don't take into account the things that you perceive as important? Sometimes, would you like to be the decision maker? Would you like to feel that the future was being shaped in a way that made sense to you?

OICES THAT DO NOT agree with me cannot take my home or my country from me. If I have no sense of home, I belong to the planet. Even when I don't like public policies, my home is still my home. My point of view belongs here. My voice is important. When I speak for myself, I also speak for others who share my values. When I am silent, I respect my need for rest and choice. I am not alone. When I feel anger or shame about what is happening, I am renewed by connecting to community. I act out of care for all beings and a fierce desire to protect life. I notice what moves me and I take action to contribute. The things that I am called to do are right for me. My contributions, public or private, are right for me.

ENVY OF OTHERS

ARE YOU SOMETIMES stunned by envy of someone else? Do you envy their accomplishments, their number of followers, income, family, wealth, beauty, community, youth, strength, health, their life? Do you just sometimes want to be this other person, instead of being yourself? Or would you like to have their privileges and see what you would do with them? Does your envy feel like a sickness inside of you that somehow needs to find its balance? After you have a bout of envy, do you have to find your way back to your own life, and does it sometimes take days, sometimes years, to find yourself again?

I AM EXACTLY RIGHT for my life. What I have to give is important. Even when it is hard for me to believe it, the things I have lived through matter. My life matters. My contributions matter. I know my own life, and I find my way back to myself when I'm knocked off balance by thinking someone else's life is better. I am here, and my dreams are waiting for me to make them real.

TECHNOLOGY

Wonderings

ARE YOU UTTERLY DEPENDENT on technology? When it stops working for you, are you frustrated and helpless? Are you annoyed by forgotten passwords and chargers, lost documents, dead hard drives, failing batteries, and looping screens that won't let you move forward? In the moments when technology disappears altogether or becomes inaccessible, is there a part of you that appreciates being suddenly without it? In the middle of the panic and overwhelm, is there an unaccustomed peace and relief? And then, when you come back online, is there a bit of desperation and anticipatory weariness with the hours of work that will be waiting for you? Would you love to have a master switch to turn off all the technology so that you could have regular breaks? Do you wish you had access to deep peace and your own sense of timing, no matter what was happening with technology?

AND MY WORK EXIST, distinct from all technology. The world and nature are here, anchoring me, even when technology fails. Meaning is separate from technology. I feel history breathing on its own, no matter what technology does. I anchor myself in my body, finding my center here inside me, rather than within a screen, a device, or a hard drive. I remember myself, my life, and my past. I know myself. My memories belong to me, not to the cloud. I accept the moments when technology fails, without panic, remembering my own center. When systems go down, I work calmly to bring things back online. I understand that tech failures happen to everyone and they do not disrupt me. They are just part of the flow.

Helplessness and Choice

EVERYTHING FEELING OUT OF CONTROL

DO YOU MISS the stability that you used to depend on? Does a lot of what's happening feel like chaos? Are your cells disoriented and unsure which direction is north? Is there a discomfort that leaves you looking for solid ground? Are you unsure where to find it? Do you sometimes want to rewind time so that things feel predictable again? Or if there never was any stability or predictability, have you lived with disquiet for so long that you wouldn't quite know what to do with yourself if the world felt solid? Are people undependable and are events spiraling out of control? Would you enjoy some moments where everything was fine, and where everyone knew that everything was fine, and they and their muscles could relax, and their throats, and smiles would come naturally, and breath would flow in and out with ease?

NO MATTER HOW UNPREDICTABLE events are, I know what I am doing, and what I am going to do. The present moment is a knowable moment, and I always know (or can find out) which direction is north. My cells are settled and calm in this present time. I ride the waves of unpredictability, sometimes with ease, and sometimes with difficulty. When the waves are rough, I am gentle with myself, and I take my time to find my balance again. I am stable, and sometimes I am unshakable.

FINANCIAL DEPENDENCE

ARE YOU TRAPPED in a living or working situation by financial considerations? Does this situation give you a home, or pay enough of the bills, so that you have a way to live? Is it killing you, and does it allow you to survive at the same time? Do you feel bewildered by life and its demands? Are you so tired from the double binds that you don't even have the energy to imagine anything better? Do you need to have faith that something better is possible, even if you can't imagine it? Do you want there to be a world in which the skills and abilities and energy that you have would be enough to support you both in terms of money and in terms of your soul? Would you love to live in that world above all else?

BELIEVE IN A LIFE where all my strengths and gifts come together, even as I experience less choice than I wish to have. I release the agreements I have with myself to be forever beholden to those who have helped me. I release the agreements I have with myself to believe my gifts are not enough. I release the agreements I have with myself to stay where it's safe, no matter the cost to myself. I release these agreements with gratitude about how they helped me survive and have self-respect. I step into my life, remembering that I have gifts and strengths that I know, and others that I don't even know yet. I am open to surprising myself. I am willing to try. I am willing to move. I address myself with respect and open myself up to choice.

 Theme 12

STEPPING INTO

CELEBRATION

CELEBRATING WHEN TIMES
ARE SO TURBULENT

Wonderings

IS IT A LITTLE ODD to find things to celebrate when the world is turned upside down? Is there a part of you that doesn't want to celebrate if things are tough for others? Do you feel heavy when you think about people struggling? Does your body protest the unfairness of the world? Do you sometimes catch a glimpse of someone else's happiness, and is there a complex response—sometimes envy, sometimes shared delight? Would you like to be lifted by your own moments of joy, to feel your heart leap and to feel your eyes sparkle? And are there tiny things that slip through the barriers? A moment with a child or with an animal, a beautiful sunrise, or fog across a valley? Would it be good to have the sense that instead of being unfair, celebration, especially joyful celebration, lightened the burden for everyone?

CELEBRATE FREELY. I release the idea that I can make the world more fair by being unhappy. I step into delight, and happiness, and joy, and awe, and I let these emotions exist in me, flowering like blossoms that then close until the next arising of good feelings. I enjoy my life. When something good happens, I fully inhale the aroma of celebration, letting it spread through my body and lighten my cells' burdens. My celebrations are small: a good movie, a deep and entertaining book, a good meal, or a beautiful sight. My celebrations are huge: the birth of a baby, two hearts finding each other, the completion of a creative act, or a good life and death. My joy, in and of itself, is a contribution to this world, lightening the shared burden and lifting other nervous systems. Life nourishes me, and I completely welcome that nourishment.

Stepping into Celebration

ACCOMPLISHMENT

Wonderings

ARE YOU HAPPY and relieved that this accomplishment went well? Do you have a complex response to professional accomplishment? Do you feel both satisfied and lonely? And if your accomplishment is completely outside the lives of most of the people you talk to, is it impossible to share the celebration? Do you miss being known in the time of the struggle, the moments when the work progresses, and in the triumph when something is completed? Is there a way that the victory might appear to be small and insignificant, or that it is incomprehensible to others, but to you it's enormous? With completion, are you so relieved that it physically lightens your body and removes burdens? And at the same time, does everything else that needs to be done come clamoring in for your attention? Would you love to have pure moments of celebration when things have been completed?

NO MATTER HOW complex my feelings are, I make sense. Each layer of feeling tells me more about how I respond to the world. I feel sad, happy, satisfied, and lonely all at once, and each feeling has a different meaning. My celebrations are complex. I enjoy my accomplishments. I know who can celebrate with me, and I share with those people, so that my celebrations grow and make me lighter. In the places where people don't know how to celebrate, I celebrate with nature, with the fruit tree blossoms in the spring, and the heavy fruit in the fall, with the pinecones and the wheat sheaves, and I am not alone.

A GOOD DAY

Wonderings

WHEN YOU HAVE a good day, does it melt into your bones and give you a sense of sweetness? Are good days remedies for all the hard days, like sun breaking through into a cloudy day? Is there sometimes a part of you that can't quite let go and enjoy the sweet moments? If this is true for you, are you protecting yourself from how brief and rare the good days are? Do you stop breathing, do you almost stop your heart from beating, so that you can keep yourself from celebrating and protect yourself from the constant disappearance of time? Would you love to have a sense of the inevitability of good days—that there would always be another one just around the corner, and that you could count on them?

WELCOME GOOD DAYS and live them fully. I make a home for them in my life. I remember the good days that are gone and let the memories of them feed me on difficult days. I anticipate the sweet days to come with faith and enjoyment. I release any contracts or stories about the number of good days I can have, and I step into the freedom to savor days filled with joy and satisfaction.

BEING LOVED

ARE YOU BEWILDERED and doubtful when another person tells you that they love you? Or that you matter to them? Are you convinced that the only reason that people notice you or care about you is because of what you can do for them? And when someone really seems to like you, do you keep looking over your shoulder to see who they are actually looking at? And do you believe that there is a way that love ought to feel, that it should include a sense of being truly seen? At the same time, does it seem impossible to ever be truly seen, and does that impossibility seem to block all the love that flows toward you? Is believing in being loved an impossible conundrum, and would you love the riddle to resolve itself inside of you, so that you could receive all different kinds of love gracefully?

I AM A SOUL and not a function. People love me for all different aspects of my being. Some people delight in me for my laughter, some for my sadness, some for my confidence, some for my humility. I understand that I have no control over love and being loved, and that often I will not recognize its sparks, because of my preconceived ideas about what love is and how it ought to feel. I am willing to be loved in all different ways by many different people, some well known and some less known by me. And when I am skeptical about the possibility of being loved, I bring affection and warmth to my skepticism and my objections, understanding the deep context of my lifetime of experience, understanding the history of betrayals and disappointments and weariness, and tenderly put my arms around it all.

Wonderings

ARE YOU SURPRISED by new, brief moments of comfort inside your own brain? Are there times now when your brain stops its relentless self-evaluation and just lets you exist? Are you settling into feeling better? Do you notice that you are starting to move from sorrow and shame to laughter and self-acceptance? Do you love the fluidity, the surprise, the fun? Is there a wonder to these moments of self-connection? Is there some sense that the emotional trauma-clearing work you are doing every day is lifting some of the continual burden that your brain and body have been carrying all these years? Do you surprise yourself with glimpses of beauty and bubbles of delight?

WELCOME AND ENJOY the way my neurons are growing and supporting me. I notice that my brain is kinder to me than it used to be. I greet myself with warmth in the morning when I wake up. I am shame-resilient and affectionate with myself when I make mistakes. I have choice in my daily life, instead of compulsions and habits. I am compelled by what I love, following the path that emerges from my passions, curiosities, and satisfactions.

AFFIRMATIONS

Wonderings

DID YOU BEGIN this book with some doubt about how much affirmations could help? Did you think they were just words? If you answered yes to many of the questions in the wonderings, was that surprising? Are you surprised by the reassurance and helpfulness of looking at your life through the lens of affirmations? Do you enjoy capturing this moment, this abundance, and the ongoing experience of being a unique self, unequalled by any other person? Is the paradoxical journey of being human, the movement ever inward, combined with the ever-widening sense of connection with the outer world, a wonder? When you read an affirmation that feels right to you, do your body and your mind settle? Do you look forward to creating your own wonderings and your own affirmations for your own themes?

MAKE SENSE. My thoughts and feelings come from my life, and they have a good place with me. I lean into invitations and good wishes for myself, for my present, and for my future. I hold the intention of growing self-kindness, and I notice and celebrate my small and large gains. I enjoy being a complex person who changes in unexpected ways. I reach for both inner growth and outer connection. I feel warmth everywhere.

TWELVE FINAL INVITATIONS

1. May I breathe deeply and feel peaceful inside, no matter how chaotic and quickly-changing the outer world is. May I take the best action for myself and the world, and still preserve my inner stillness. May I hold with compassion the ways that my inner world and the outer world come together.

2. May I stay well, and remember my best possible health as my body's home. May I be kind, patient, and affectionate with myself when I am ill. May I continually return to self-accompaniment, no matter what state my health is in.

3. May I enjoy myself in both company and when I am alone. May I feel my community with me even when I am separated from it. May I experience being met with authentic welcome in my life.

4. May I find a good path for contribution and sustainability, even abundance, in my life. May I do work

that I enjoy, and that has meaning for me. May I value my own gifts and strengths, and be supported to find their best expression.

5. May the people I love live well, with continual resilience. May I know peace about the people I care about. May I contribute to them in ways that feel good, with a sense of humor, and may I experience mutuality and interdependence.

6. May I mourn well for the people I miss, and may I honor them, and myself, with my mourning. May I remember all the warmth that I have received from others and carry it with me. May I be gentle with myself when I do not want the world to change.

7. May I have moments when I see what is happening to our world with clarity, and be able to bear it. When pain and mourning overwhelm me, may I know that I share this mourning with millions of others, and may I let the pain move through me and support my action, rather than stopping my responsiveness and my care.

8. May I have a great affection for my own grouchiness. May others feel my care for them, even when I am irritable and grumpy. May I have the patience and warmth for myself and others to support me in remaining connected even though I am so very human.

9. May I be warm with myself when I am blocked. May I recognize my own unique gifts and have faith in them. May I trust my own timing and emergence.

10. May I remember that I can stand outside myself and look at myself with compassion, even when depression threatens. May I remember the colors of the world at the moments when I cannot see them. May life's meaning find me, even when I cannot find it.

11. May I live with a sense of choice. May I use my choice for my well-being and for the well-being of those whose life I touch. May I touch life's abundance and generosity. May I mourn well the places where choice is still inaccessible to me.

12. May I know the power and importance of celebration, held simultaneously with mourning. May I lighten my own and others' burdens with moments of appreciation and joy. May I be surprised by celebration of small and large things, as they arise.

Author's Closing:
What Next?

THIS BOOK has taken us on a brain-changing and life-changing journey. It has invited us to acknowledge some of the complex layers of emotion that we humans feel about living in a world filled with tumult. And it has also invited us into a relationship with presence and hope, and with our best qualities and deepest values, despite our tumultuous times.

Along the way, we've been supporting the growth of new neural connections—connections that provide our brains with resilience, persistence, and grace. Sometimes the word "resilience" is used as if it meant the capacity to be unchanged by stress, but in fact researchers are discovering that resilient brains are three times more changed by stressful circumstances than nonresilient brains are. These researchers have found that sensitivity and adaptation are the foundations of resilience, rather than stoicism. Strangely, what this implies is that sensitivity is our resilience superpower.

This book is just a starting point for you on your own brain-change journey. There are many things that we have complex feelings about, many experiences that need self-accompaniment, and many painful messages that we carry, all of which need their own wonderings and affirmations.

If you feel shy or hesitant about starting to write your own affirmations, please allow me to accompany you by sharing how it was for me to embark on writing this book. I have loved writing this book so much. But the writing of it took me into intense vulnerability. It is a direct offering of resonance, unshielded by neuroscience, without the clothing of process work. You may feel vulnerable or exposed, so I share with you some glimpses of how I spoke to myself as I started to write, in the hope that it will support you. "Just begin. And if shame arises, be kind to it and to yourself in feeling it. Acknowledge your vulnerability and keep on going. Consult your body when it feels right, if it feels right. Your body can help guide you through the issues you want to resolve and can let you know about your deepest hopes and values. If your body doesn't speak to you, just follow your thoughts."

If this book has interested you in how your life experiences have shaped your brain's voice, and you want to learn more about what relational neuroscience has to tell you about making your brain a good place to live, I invite you to read my books *Your Resonant Self: Guided Meditations and Exercises to Engage Your Brain's Capacity for Healing* and *Your Resonant Self Workbook: From Self-Sabotage to Self-Care.* The first book, *Your Resonant Self,* is a guided tour along the journey of making your brain a good place to live. The workbook is all about changing and releasing the agreements we make with ourselves, and the deep needs we are meeting related to self-sabotage and addiction. Together, these books provide a comprehensive, gentle, and warm brain-change experience.

Thank you so much for being on this brain-change journey with me—I wish you the very best in our tumultuous world. May we all turn toward ourselves and our planet with warmth and compassion as we make our way through our lives.

Notes

x   *Research shows us that we find affirmations pleasurable . . .*

Cascio, C. N., O'Donnell, M. B., Tinney, F. J., Lieberman, M. D., Taylor, S. E., Strecher, V. J., & Falk, E. B. (2015). Self-affirmation activates brain systems associated with self-related processing and reward and is reinforced by future orientation. *Social Cognitive and Affective Neuroscience, 11*(4), 621–629. doi:10.1093/scan/nsv136

xi   *They have been shown to help people move out of immobilization and into action . . .*

Cascio et al., 2015; Cohen, G. L., & Sherman, D. K. (2014). The psychology of change: Self-affirmation and social psychological intervention. *Annual Review of Psychology, 65*, 333–371.

175   *Sometimes the word "resilience" is used as if it meant the capacity to be unchanged by stress . . .*

Krishnan, V., Han, M., Graham, D. L., Berton, O., Renthal, W., Russo, S. J., Laplant, Q., Graham, A., Lutter, M., Lagace, D. C., Ghose, S., Reister, R., Tannous, P., Green, T. A., Neve, R. L., Chakravarty, S., Kumar, A., Eisch, A. J., Self, D. W., Lee, F. S., Tamminga, C. A., Cooper, D. C., Gershenfeld, H. K., & Nestler, E. J. (2007). Molecular adaptations underlying susceptibility and resistance to social defeat in brain reward regions. *Cell, 131*(2), 391–404. doi:10.1016/j.cell.2007.09.018